A Day in the Life: Rain Forest Animals

Anaconda

Anita Ganeri

Heinemann Library
Chicago, IL

www.heinemannraintree.com
Visit our website to find out
more information about
Heinemann-Raintree books.

To order:
☎ Phone 888-454-2279
🖳 Visit www.heinemannraintree.com
to browse our catalog and order online.

©2011 Heinemann Library
an imprint of Capstone Global Library, LLC
Chicago, Illinois

Edited by Nancy Dickmann, Rebecca Rissman, and
Catherine Veitch
Designed by Steve Mead
Picture research by Mica Brancic
Originated by Capstone Global Library
Printed and bound in China by South China Printing
Company Ltd

14 13 12 11 10
10 9 8 7 6 5 4 3 2

**Library of Congress Cataloging-in-
Publication Data**
Ganeri, Anita, 1961-
  Anaconda / Anita Ganeri.—1st ed.
    p. cm.—(A day in the life. Rain forest animals)
  Includes bibliographical references and index.
  ISBN 978-1-4329-4112-3 (hc)—ISBN 978-1-4329-4123-9
(pb) 1. Anaconda—Juvenile literature. I. Title.
  QL666.O63G36 2011
  597.96'7—dc22   2010001135

Acknowledgments
We would like to thank the following for permission to
reproduce photographs: Ardea p. 16 (Francois Gohier);
Corbis p. 17 (© Joe McDonald); Getty Images p. 22 (Dorling
Kindersley); FLPA pp. 6 (Minden Pictures/Claus Meyer), 9, 18,
23 swamp (Jurgen & Christine Sohns), 13 (Minden Pictures/
Heidi & Hans-Juergen Koch); Photolibrary pp. 4 (Animals
Animals/Francois Savigny), 5, 23 reptile (First Light Associated
Photographers/Philippe Henry), 7, 23 camouflage (age
fotostock/Morales Morales), 14, 23 capybara (F1 Online/
Ritterbach Ritterbach), 20 (age fotostock/Berndt Fischer), 21
(Juniors Bildarchiv); Photolibrary [Rex Features] p. 19
(age fotostock/Morales Morales); Photoshot/NHPA pp. 10,
11, 12, 15, 23 jaws, 23 prey; Shutterstock p. 23 rain forest
(© Szefei).

Cover photograph of a green anaconda reproduced with
permission of Photolibrary (Animals Animals/Austin
J Stevens).

Back cover photographs of (left) a yellow anaconda
constricting prey reproduced with permission of Photoshot
(NHPA); and (right) a green anaconda (Eunectes murinus)
reproduced with permission of FLPA (Minden Pictures/Heidi
& Hans-Juergen).

We would like to thank Michael Bright for his invaluable help
in the preparation of this book.

Every effort has been made to contact copyright holders
of material reproduced in this book. Any omissions will
be rectified in subsequent printings if notice is given to
the publisher.

Contents

Some words are in bold, **like this**. You can find them in the glossary on page 23.

What Is an Anaconda?

An anaconda is a kind of snake.

All snakes have long, tube-shaped bodies with a head at one end and a tail at the other.

alligator

Anacondas and other snakes belong to a group of animals called **reptiles**.

Alligators, crocodiles, lizards, turtles, and tortoises are also reptiles.

What Do Anacondas Look Like?

An anaconda has a very long, thick body.

An adult anaconda can grow to be almost as long as a school bus.

An anaconda's skin is dark green or yellow with a pattern of large, black spots.

This helps to **camouflage** the snake.

South America

Anacondas live in the **rain forests** of South America.

It is warm and wet in the rain forest all year long.

Anacondas like to live in slow-moving streams and **swamps** in the rain forest.

They spend most of their time in the water.

What Do Anacondas Do at Night?

At night, anacondas hunt for food.

They lie in the water and wait for their **prey**.

prey

The anaconda grabs its prey in its **jaws**.

It coils, or wraps, its body around the prey and squeezes it to death.

Can Anacondas Swim?

An anaconda can swim very fast to catch its **prey**.

It curves its body from side to side, pushing the water behind it.

nostril

eye

An anaconda's eyes and nostrils are on the top of its head.

This helps it to see and breathe while it is swimming or floating in the water.

What Do Anacondas Eat?

capybaras

Anacondas hunt other **rain forest** animals, such as fish, birds, and frogs.

Large anacondas can catch bigger animals, such as **capybaras**.

jaws

An anaconda swallows its **prey** whole, head first.

Its **jaws** are held together by stretchy bands so it can open its mouth very wide.

What Do Anacondas Do after Feeding?

food

It takes an anaconda a long time to take in food.

It lies on a riverbank or in the water, hardly moving at all.

After a big meal, an anaconda may not need to eat again for several weeks or even months.

Then it goes hunting again.

What Do Baby Anacondas Look Like?

baby

Many snakes lay eggs, but anacondas have babies that look like small adults.

A female anaconda has up to 40 babies at a time.

Baby anacondas are born in the water at night.

Then their mother swims away and leaves them alone.

What Do Anacondas Do During the Day?

An anaconda spends the day resting and sleeping.

It cannot close its eyes because it does not have eyelids.

The anaconda's eyes are covered with see-through skin.

This makes its eyes look like they are staring.

Anaconda Body Map

body

tongue

eye

head

tail

skin

Glossary

 **camouflage** color or patterns of an animal's fur or skin that help it to hide

 **capybara** rain forest animal that looks like a large guinea pig

 **jaws** top and bottom parts of the mouth

 **prey** animal that is hunted by other animals for food

 **rain forest** thick forest with very tall trees and a lot of rain

 **reptile** animal that has scaly skin, such as snakes and crocodiles

 **swamp** piece of land that is often covered by water

Find Out More

Books

Mattern, Joanne. *Anacondas.* Mankako, MN: Capstone
   Press, 2009.
Polydoros, Lori. *Anacondas: On the Hunt.* Mankato, MN:
   Capstone Press, 2010.

Websites

www.sandiegozoo.org/animalbytes/t-boa.html
www.zoo.org/animal-facts/anaconda

Index